Becoming America's Stories presents ...

Becoming America's Food Stories

A collection of reminiscences and recipes

Antoinette Truglio Martin

Becoming America's Food Stories

Copyright © 2020 by Antoinette Truglio Martin

All rights reserved.

Published by Red Penguin Books

Bellerose Village, New York

Library of Congress Control Number: 2020922729

ISBN

Digital 978-1-952859-72-4

Print 978-1-952859-71-7 / 978-1-952859-76-2 / 978-1-952859-77-9

No part of this book may be reproduced in any form or by any electronic or mechanical means, including information storage and retrieval systems, without written permission from the author, except for the use of brief quotations in a book review.

CONTENTS

Introduction vii

Part I
MORE THAN MACARONI

1. Daily Bread 3
2. Papa's Joy 7
3. Puttanesca Sauce 11
4. It's Sauce-Not Gravy 15
5. Meatballs on a Fork 19
6. Special Occasion Braciole 23

Part II
FISH

7. Grandma's Clam Chowder 29
8. A Fish Story 35

Part III
EGGPLANT

9. Parm & Stacks 41
10. Caponata 47
11. Uncle Tom's Heartburn 53

Part IV
VEGGIES, EGGS, AND A SANDWICH

12. Converting the Cauliflower Shunners 61
13. Bread Crumbs 65
14. Artichokes 69
15. Breakfast with Great Grandma 75
16. Seamless Sandwich 79

Part V
SOUPS AND STEWS
17. Versatile Chicken Soup — 87
18. "Stick To Your Ribs" Comfort — 93

Part VI
DESSERT
19. What's for Dessert? — 103
20. Mrs. Goldberg's Knot Surprises — 109

Acknowledgments — 113
About the Author — 115

For my parents, Diana and Bill Truglio—the best mom and dad ever.

INTRODUCTION

"If you don't cook with love, you have to get out of the kitchen!"

First, I am not a trained chef nor a student of the culinary arts or an influencer lifestyle-ist. I am a good home cook with a great appetite for hearty food. I have witnessed the creation of favorite recipes in friends' kitchens and have learned from the best—my mom, grandma, and mother-in-law, Helga Martin, who put a German flare to her meals.

Like so many Americans, my family's American history began on Ellis Island and the Little Italy neighborhoods of the Lower East Side tenements when the 20th century was young. My Sicilian and southern Italian great-grandparents and grandparents worked hard, took risks, and sacrificed to make America their home. They were the backbone of America's labor force. Their journeys were harrowing, brave, adventurous, sad and joyful. Their histories became part of America's stories.

Tales shared through and within generations define our heritage, provide us with empathy over transgressions, and celebrate our adventures. They are as essential as the food that feeds our bodies. Stories fuel our souls. Family food stories are especially rich.

I am blessed with a large, loud and loving family tribe. We enjoy our Sunday dinners and special occasions together. The stories of our ancestors were and still are told around the dinner table. Sitting down surrounded by multi-generations of relations was just as sustaining as the familiar foods served. The memories added spice to our nourishment. Versions of the truth are flushed out as we pass the sauce, laugh out loud, sip wine and dab stained lips.

I included favorite recipes to accompany the stories. The recipes that evolved from the immigration experience to today may differ in procedures, but share taste preferences and a comfort.

It should be noted that when I cook, I seldom measure. In fact, the family cooks before me did not measure. The amounts shown are approximations. Interpret "drizzle", "splash", "pinch" to your smell and taste preferences and the size of your family.

Grab a glass of wine. Enjoy the reminiscences, recipes, and love.

Mom and Dad's 60th Anniversary

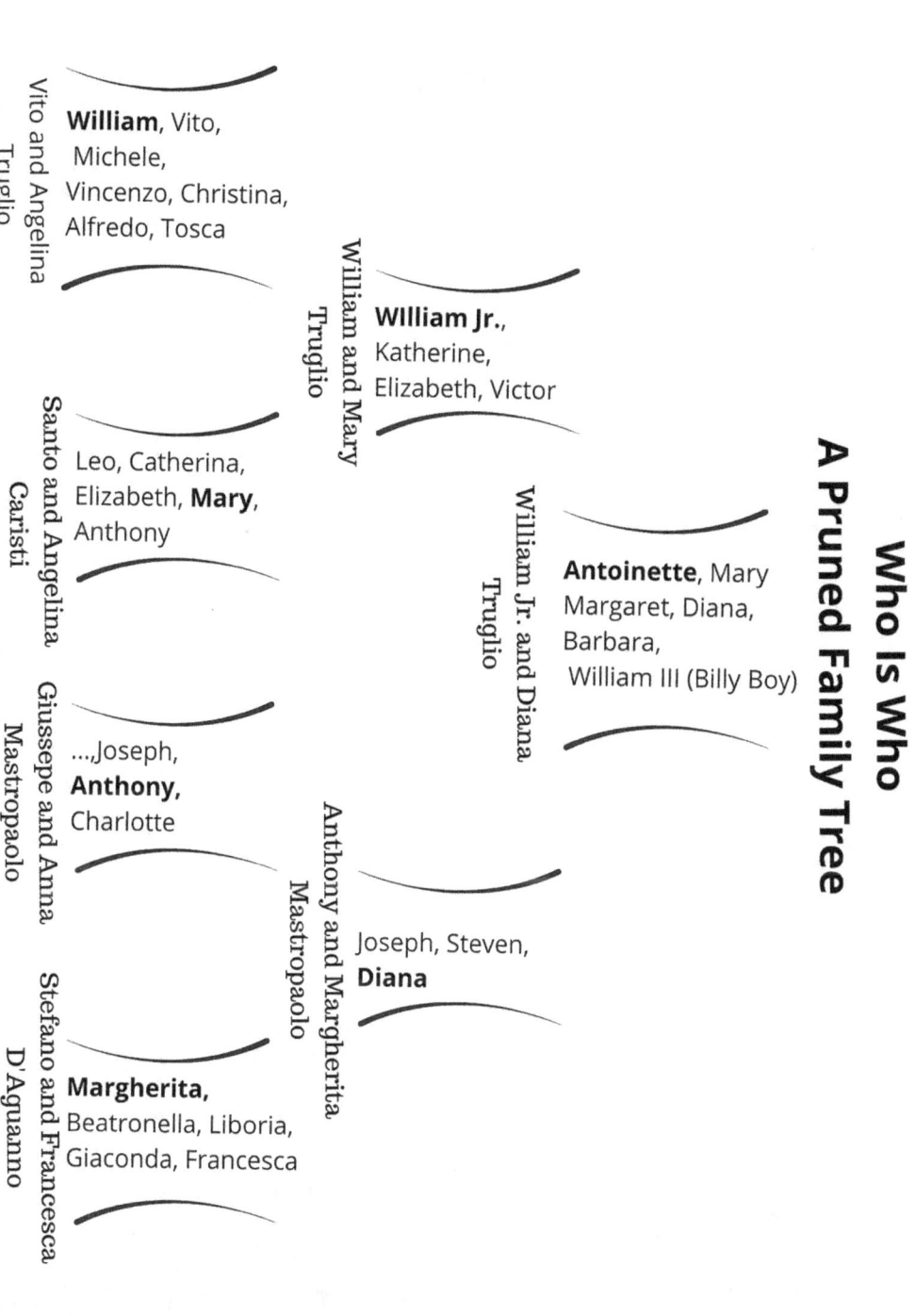

I

MORE THAN MACARONI

1

DAILY BREAD

As stated in *Daily Bread*, my historical fiction novel that is based on my Grandma Mastropaolo's childhood, bread was an essential food that accompanied meals. As a child, my grandmother learned how to bake bread from the Jewish baker on the corner of Hester Street who allowed children to commit to a daily bread baking routine.

Grandma did not favor cooking. Widowed early in life, she returned to the factory workforce to support herself and children. She was lucky to live with or close to her parents and sisters who took care of the daily shopping, meals and childcare.

Her one specialty, though, was bread. When she visited us, her mission was to clean and organize my mother's kitchen and bake bread and dozens of rolls. Grandma baked plain white breads that were amazing with a pat of butter or dipped in sauce.

My mom also baked bread when I was a kid. She pulled sweet whole wheat, rye, and pumpernickel loaves out of the oven. There was nothing better than coming home to the aroma of bread baking. Years ago, I had a wonderful bread-making machine that had a beautiful loaf waiting for my family at the end of a long school and work day. It was quickly devoured before I could start cooking dinner.

Unfortunately, eating a loaf or two of freshly baked bread each day is not a healthy option. The bread machine and packs of yeast faded from the kitchen.

My sister, Diana, is most patient and attentive with hand kneading and baking bread. This is her recollection of Grandma Mastropaolo's bread. It is not the same bread Grandma baked as a child in the basement of the Jewish bakery—it's better.

Great Grandma and Grandma

GRANDMA'S BREAD

- 4 cups all-purpose unbleached flour
- 1 ½ cups of water, warm to slightly hot to the touch
- 1 package of yeast
- 1 tablespoon sugar
- 1 teaspoon salt
- 3 tablespoons butter melted but not too hot

Stir the yeast and sugar in the water. Let the water sit for approximately 8-10 minutes to allow the yeast to activate. The water should become bubbly.

Combine the flour and salt in a bowl. Make an indent or well in the middle of the flour mixture. Add the butter and water while stirring with a wooden spoon.

Knead the dough, adding flour as needed. It should be somewhat sticky to your hand but not wet. Shape the dough into a round mound and smear it with Crisco or butter. Cover the bowl with a towel and place it in a warm spot. Let it rise for approximately 3-4 hours.

Form the bread on a greased or buttered cookie sheet. Let rise for approximately 45 minutes to an hour.

Bake in a 350° oven for 45-50 minutes or until it sounds hollow when tapped.

2

PAPA'S JOY

Aunt Tosca described her father, Papa Truglio, as a somber man especially when compared to his party-loving wife, sons, daughters, and grandchildren. While the crowd played cards, sang songs and talked over each other, Papa quietly sat at the table. He would, however, perk up when moved to cook his favorite food that brought him simple joy.

The Country House

During the post-WWII summers, the Truglio families congregated at the Country House, a small cottage on the South Shore of Long Island where the Truglios of all ages played, fish, and swam. It was a great escape from the stuffy Brooklyn streets and homes. Many times, three to five families bunked in together for non-stop summer fun. The nights were as epic as the days and meals were like sporting events, especially on Sundays.

Sunday dinner began after church and continued until there was almost nothing left. The day set into the night when the last piece of cake and dredges of coffee were served, but the conversations and laughter continued into the evening. Grandpa Truglio played the piano while the uncles and aunts sang and danced. Bare-chested children hung over uncles' shoulders, watching hands of cards play out. Tag games overflowed from the yard into the house and up the stairs. Mama and the aunts washed and dried dishes without a moment of silence between them.

Papa watched, sipped coffee and nodded. Finally he stood up and called out, "Who wants spaghetti aglio e olio?

"Papa, we just ate. You can't be hungry. The dishes are done."

"I want spaghetti aglio e olio. I'll cook a little bit."

As he waited for the pot of water to boil, he chopped cloves of garlic.

"Papa, make a little for me," said one uncle.

The garlic simmered in a pan with olive oil.

"I'll have some, too, Papa," said another.

The little house filled with the intense aroma of garlic sautéing in oil.

"We want some, Papa. Make enough for us," the children called out.

Papa boiled two pounds of spaghetti, drained it, then tossed in the aglio e olio. Spaghetti aglio e olio filled mismatched bowls around the family table. Everyone wanted a sprinkle of grated cheese on top. Papa beamed, happy to be in the company of his noisy brood.

"It was a beautiful time with everyone together singing, eating, and enjoying each other," reminisced Aunt Tosca.

Papa and grandson, Larry

SPAGHETTI AGLIO E OLIO

- fresh garlic
- olive oil
- spaghetti

While the spaghetti cooks in a pot of boiling water with a dash of salt added, chop the garlic. If you really like it, chop a whole head of garlic. Add olive oil to a heated pan and sauté the garlic until a little brown and very fragrant. Keep a careful eye on the pan as garlic browns quickly. Strain the cooked spaghetti, but leave a bit of pasta water at the bottom of the pot. Put the spaghetti back in the pot and toss the oil and garlic incorporating the pasta water. Served hot with sprinkles of favorite grated cheese.

3

PUTTANESCA SAUCE

Puttanesca sauce has several legends. It was said to have been cooked for soldiers marching through villages, was a chef's assistant's invention when an important customer demanded immediate food after the chef had gone home, or a quick dish women of ill repute prepared and ate between their clients' appointments. In all of the versions, the commonality was that the sauce was made in haste.

I do not remember any of my grandmothers cooking or talking about puttanesca sauce. It might have been too fishy with the smelly anchovies. It was certainly too salty for my mom to allow my dad to eat. She always watched his salt intake.

Apparently, Uncle Phil is known for his puttanesca sauce. He shows off his culinary skills by whipping up a pan of sauce while the macaroni boils in a pot. He is very generous with anchovies, olives, and capers. In no time, the pan of puttanesca sauce is tossed into a bowl of spaghetti or linguini. Simple. Quick. Delicious.

Linguine with Puttanesca Sauce

Uncle Phil's Macaroni and Puttanesca Sauce

Adjust the amounts of each ingredient to your taste preferences.

- favorite macaroni (Uncle Phil prefers linguini)
- olive oil
- garlic
- anchovies packed in oil
- 14.5 oz. can of diced tomatoes
- kalamata olives
- onion
- ¼-½ cup of capers

Put a pot of water up to boil for the macaroni. Chop garlic, olives, and onion. Cut the anchovies in half or thirds.

Drizzle olive oil in a pan. Sauté the garlic until fragrant. Add diced tomatoes, anchovies, olives, and onion and cook until desired consistency.

Once the macaroni is boiled and rinsed, the sauce should be ready. If the sauce is too thick, ladle in a scoop of macaroni water to loosen it up. Toss the sauce in the macaroni. Add capers. Hurry up and eat.

Aunt Kay and Uncle Phil

4

IT'S SAUCE-NOT GRAVY

I grew up on sauce. Tomato sauce simmered on Sundays. A big pot cooked on the stove most of the day so that there was plenty of sauce leftover for the week.

My parents remembered how preserving tomatoes into sauce took over kitchens and put everyone to work. In August, Dad's Uncle Leo and Nonno came home with baskets of tomatoes. Nonna cleaned, cooked down the tomatoes, and strained out the seeds, skins, and pulp in her tight kitchen in August's heat. Instead of buying mason jars, the cooked tomatoes were funneled into empty wine bottles and placed in another pot of boiling water to cook some more. Bottlecaps were crimped on top of the bottles, and the kids carefully wrapped them in newspapers. Dad's Brooklyn home had a basement that housed shelves of jarred goods. Once or twice a year, a "bad" bottle exploded, waking everyone to what sounded like a shotgun.

Mom's grandmother's Brooklyn basement was also cool and perfect for storing foods for the winter. She recalled how she followed her grandmother's orders to let a huge pan of tomatoes dry in the heat and sun on the driveway to make tomato paste, the thickening for the sauce.

No one can argue that fresh tomatoes that had been blanched, skinned, seeded, and jarred are the best base for sauce. But tomato season is short and jarring tomatoes in the heat of the summer is torture. These days, whole and crushed canned tomatoes suffice.

Sauce evolved with time. In the "old" days, a simmering pot had to be guarded all day to save from burning the bottom. I believed for the longest time household matriarchs got special dispensation from missing Sunday Mass because they had to cook the sauce.

I cook my sauce in a heavy Dutch oven, but if I have a busy day ahead I set up a crockpot, allowing it to bubble all day without worrying about burnt pot bottoms and stirring. Mom and Grandma put meat leftovers from the week in their sauce. My daughters shunned meat, so my sauce was vegetarian-friendly. Mom and Grandma used dried parsley, basil, and oregano to flavor the sauce. I like to season my sauce with fresh herbs, roasted garlic, and homemade pesto.

The sauce is folded into bowls of linguine and ziti and topped on lasagna and manicotti. At my family's table, sauce functions beyond the gravy. In the early courtship years, my German husband, Matt, endured Sunday dinner culture shock. Eyebrows raised when he requested butter for his bread and a separate plate for salad. He almost gasped when the rest of us—my parents, sisters, brother, Grandma, and Aunt Lil, served themselves salad on their macaroni plates and ladled the sauce on top. A sprinkle of cheese added color and taste.

Sauce—better than gravy or salad dressing.

Sunday Sauce

SUNDAY SAUCE

- olive oil
- finely chopped fresh garlic or roasted garlic
- finely chopped onion, ½ fennel bulb, red or green peppers
- 3 cans of crushed tomatoes (28 oz each)
- dried or freshly chopped parsley, oregano, basil
- dash of hot red pepper flakes
- bay leaf
- salt and pepper to taste

Sauté garlic in the olive oil until fragrant. Add chopped onions, fennel, and peppers until onions are transparent. Add the cans of tomatoes, dried or fresh herbs, and the bay leaf. Salt and pepper to taste. Cook and stir gently. The longer it gently simmers, the more flavor rendered and the house smells like Sunday. Add meats or cooked vegetables. Served over a favorite macaroni. Sprinkle with parmesan or Pecorino grated cheese.

Sunday sauce with meatballs in a crockpot

5

MEATBALLS ON A FORK

Sundays were macaroni and meatball days. Mom would start the sauce first thing in the morning. She claimed that my little brother, Billy Boy, wouldn't know the next day was Monday if he didn't have macaroni and meatballs on Sunday.

When I was a kid, Sundays were spent in Brooklyn at Grandma Truglio's. The staircase and second floor flat were filled with the aromas of garlic, tomatoes, the trinity (oregano, basil, and parsley), and a roast. Grandma chopped, pinched, stirred, rolled meatballs, and checked the oven throughout the morning. Company was coming for a day of celebrating anything and eating. An endless parade of dishes filled with macaroni, assorted vegetables, and meats adorned the dining room table.

My mom took on this role when Grandma moved from Brooklyn to Long Island. The sauce was put up first thing in the morning. I would wake up to the wafts of garlic and onion. Mom made the meatballs, cleaned whatever vegetable she had planned as a side dish, and dressed the roast. Company was coming. Mom was determined to feed the masses. If there were no leftovers, then someone surely went home hungry.

Once the meatballs were mixed, rolled, then baked, they simmered in the sauce. You could smell the inviting warmth all day. Heaven.

Lunchtime never happened on Sundays. Dinner started at about 2:00 in the afternoon. If someone got hungry before company arrived, before the cheese, olives, and crackers came out, they had to ask Mom what there was to eat. The last thing Mom wanted to do was to stop the prepping and make a cranky kid or hungry husband a sandwich. Instead, Mom took a fork and stabbed a meatball simmering in the pot of sauce. She placed a paper towel under the dripping prize.

"Eat this. Don't make a mess!" she instructed. A meatball on a fork was the best pre-appetizer.

Through the years, Mom's grandchildren came to know the Sunday dinner routine. Mom's most cherished compliment was when her grandson, Michael, walked into her house and announced, "It smells like Sunday at Grandma's!" His reward was a kiss and a meatball on a fork. To this day, the routine still occurs.

Meatball recipes evolved over the years. Most of my sisters use chopped beef, seasoned bread crumbs, milk, or water. My cousin, Lorraine, adds raisins as her Sicilian grandmother had done. Some roll huge meatballs, like a mini meatloaf, while others fashion baby-size spheres. It is a personal preference dictated by what the cook's family craves.

Sunday spaghetti and meatballs

SUNDAY MEATBALLS

- 1 to 1½ -pound of chopped beef and pork. If there was a sale, I would splurge on the beef, pork, and veal package.
- finely chopped ½ onion and 2 cloves of garlic (roasted garlic is best)
- olive oil
- seasoned bread crumbs
- grated parmesan or romano cheese
- 1 egg
- pesto
- salt and pepper to taste
- oregano and parsley (if fresh, chop very fine or use a mini food processor to pulverize with a bit of oil)

Sauté chopped onion and roasted garlic in a splash of olive oil until the onions are translucent. Let it cool.

Add the egg to the meat, mix. Add the sautéed onions, garlic, the oregano, parsley, salt, and pepper. Incorporate equal amounts of bread crumbs and cheese, and handmix everything until you reach the desired texture.

Take a palm-size portion of the meat mixture, roll into a ball, and place on a cookie tray.

Bake the meatballs in a 350°F oven for about 20-30 minutes. Let cool in a bowl with paper towels to absorb excess fat. Place the meatballs into a pot of sauce.

Fend off anyone claiming to be a taste tester unless they earned a meatball on a fork.

Classic meatball on a fork.

6

SPECIAL OCCASION BRACIOLE

Just talking about the possibility of cooking braciole results in raised eyebrows and amorous sighs. The spoken thoughts of braciole possibilities are quickly followed by questions of when and where. Bracioles were on holiday menus, namely Christmas and Thanksgiving (turkey was always a second thought on the family's Thanksgiving table). Grandma Truglio's bracioles were tender enough to cut with a fork. The hard-boiled egg in the center of the rolled meat inspired surprise with the pop of color against the cooked meat. My mother-in-law wrapped a pickle with bacon and mustard in her rouladen—a German version of braciole. Either way, the meat rolls were saved for special occasions since they were labor-intensive and expensive.

My sister, Diana, recreated Grandma Truglio's braciole. She asked our mother for instructions and called Aunt Linda and Uncle Vic for tips. Uncle Vic called out from the other side of the room that she should make sure the braciole cooks in the sauce for a long time (how long is a guess).

BRACIOLE

- 4 thinly sliced top round steak cutlets or pork cutlets
- 4 3-minute boiled eggs, peeled

Filling

- ¾ cup Italian seasoned bread crumbs
- ½ cup grated Parmigiano Reggiano cheese
- 2 garlic cloves crushed
- ½ teaspoon salt
- 1 teaspoon pepper
- 2 tablespoons olive oil

In a small bowl combine bread crumbs, grated cheese, garlic, salt, pepper and olive oil.

SPECIAL OCCASION BRACIOLE | 25

Pound meat to approximately ¼ inch thick. Sprinkle olive oil on the top. Spoon a layer of filling on the pounded steak. Put one boiled egg on one end of the cutlet and roll. Tie with butcher string.

Heat a small pan on a medium to medium-high heat. Add olive oil. Braise the bracioles.

Add the braciole to your favorite tomato sauce. Cook on low for at least 3 hours.

(The longer they cook in the sauce the more tender they become.)

II

FISH

7

GRANDMA'S CLAM CHOWDER

Grandma Truglio was an excellent cook—not a fancy gourmet chef, but a home cook who could turn ingredients into an epic meal. The stairwell to her second floor flat in Brooklyn heralded the warmth and goodness waiting behind her door. She enveloped each of her visitors with big arm hugs and kisses.

Grandma did not teach anyone how to cook. You had to be in her kitchen, sipping Sanka instant decaf coffee (coffee was not her specialty), chatting about anything while observing her techniques. She was generous with tips and shortcuts, and there was a wide smile as she stirred. I loved reaching up to the pot with the heel of Italian bread to dip in the sauce. Cooking for family was her joy. When I inherited one of her cookbooks titled *The All Italian Cookbook*, I was disappointed to find that she did not leave notes. She used it for ideas, not directions.

Grandma did not measure. She cooked by feel, taste, and smell. She understood food. When we went grocery shopping together, she looked for specific brands of oil and canned tomatoes and sorted through the green beans, squeezed onions, and smelled the garlic bulbs. The deli clerks knew how she liked the prosciutto sliced and Locatelli cheese grated.

Grandma knew the nutritional value of every food that came across her counter. When I was pregnant with my first child and incredibly nauseous consuming the prescribed amount of milk and yogurt (I was lactose intolerant before it became fashionable), I worried that my baby's bones would suffer from my neglect. Grandma blanched broccoli, cooled it in time so that the color remained bright and the texture crisp. She baked the broccoli with a sprinkle of grated Pecorino Romano cheese (I later learned that this cheese was made from sheep milk).

"There is more calcium in one broccoli spear then in a quart of milk," she claimed.

It was delicious. My baby was born healthy and strong.

Every summer my parents hosted a family picnic. Anywhere from seventy to one hundred relations, and those we have known so long they may as well be related, would show up in my parents' backyard. Everyone brought something—potluck Truglio style. Aunt Linda's sausage and peppers, my mother-in-law's potato salad, speciality sausage from Jersey, Brooklyn bread, Aunt Kay's lasagna.

Grandma cooked her clam chowder in her largest pot. The taste was robust and smoky, and there was an abundance of fresh clams. It was a perfect evening nosh after a fun day playing bocce, swimming and water skiing in the bay, and catching up with aunts, uncles, and cousins. Grandma's Clam Chowder was a favorite for all except Grandma. She did not care for any of the seafood or the fish she cooked.

"Grandma, how can you cook these amazing calamari, baked blowfish, and scungilli dishes without tasting or liking them?"

"I know how it should smell and there is always someone tasting for me," she replied. Then she would laugh.

I sat in her kitchen sipping her Sanka instant coffee while watching her make the chowder several times. One time, I smartly wrote down the ingredients and sequence. I noted quantities and proportions. When Grandma passed, it was all I had to recreate Grandma's Clam Chowder. The first attempts failed. Everyone had suggestions. I eventually learned to trust my smell and taste memory. I left the measuring spoons in the drawer and remembered to smile while I stirred.

Over the years the chowder has evolved to my own concoction. I use diced tomatoes instead of tomato juice, my home-made pesto, and roasted garlic. No matter how much the chowder has changed, it is still called Grandma's Clam Chowder. I take it as a beloved compliment.

The Grandmas

GRANDMA'S CLAM CHOWDER ALA ANTOINETTE

- bacon (as much as you want)
- finely diced celery or fennel, onion, red pepper, and zucchini
- Yukon potatoes peeled and diced
- canned diced tomatoes
- chicken or vegetable broth
- pesto
- garlic, preferably roasted, finely diced
- red pepper flakes, pepper, salt, and oregano

GRANDMA'S CLAM CHOWDER | 33

- 12-18 cherry stone or chowder size clams shucked and chopped—save the juice
- chopped parsley

Cook the bacon until crispy in the soup pot. Remove the bacon but keep the fat in the pot. Chop the bacon into bits and set aside.

Use the fat from the bacon to sauté the celery or fennel, garlic, onion, red pepper, zucchini, and potatoes until the onion is translucent.

Pour equal amounts of broth and canned tomatoes, then add pesto, oregano, and bacon. Season with salt, pepper, and red pepper flakes to taste.

Simmer until vegetables are softened and tomatoes taste done.

Add the clams and their juice. Adjust the consistency with water or broth.

Add parsley. Simmer for a while. Salt and season to taste.

Grandma's Clam Chowder is wonderful over a piece of crusty bread and topped with a sprinkle of grated Pecorino Romano cheese.

Annual Family Picnic 1984

8

A FISH STORY

There is a treasure trove of fish stories around my family's table. Fishing has and still is a great family pastime that is shared among the generations of men, women and children.

The love of the sea and the need to hold a fishing pole probably stemmed from the family's Sicilian and southern Italian roots. If they didn't farm or cut stone, they fished. The original homes most of the ancestors came from were in fishing villages. They weaved nets, set lines, and launched dories each morning and returned at the end of the day with the bounty.

My dad and uncles kept boats in varying degrees of repair and seaworthiness just so we could all get to a beach or go fishing. As small children, my siblings, cousins, and I were given some form of a fishing pole to pull in our catch. Snappers and blowfish were in abundance back then. We all got caught up in the excitement and awe of the fascinating creatures, especially the blowfish that blew up onto a prickly ball and made croaking sounds.

Fish dishes were always on the family weekly menu. We Catholics marked Fridays as fish day—no meat, but during the summer, fish meals showed up more frequently. Grandma Truglio, who would not eat the incredible fish and seafood dishes she cooked, made trays of baked blowfish tails, snappers, and bluefish we had caught. The summer table talk swelled with fish tales.

The Sunfish story has a few versions but Aunt Marsha told the best one. One summer afternoon my dad and uncles putt-putt home from a day of fishing off the Fire Island inlet. They had strapped a two-hundred-pound sunfish to the side of the 25' Higgins.

A sunfish is a peculiar fish. Their huge bodies look like a giant flat head with a short tail. The fins are seemingly too small and narrow to enable a graceful swim or quick get away from predators. Sunfish can be spotted on the ocean surface, carelessly flopping their pectoral fins while slurping jellyfish.

My dad and uncles had never seen a sunfish before and thought the catch would provide days of meals. At the time, the sunfish was the biggest fish they had ever caught and there was nothing better than actual proof of their incredible fish story. They pulled into the canal behind Uncle Tom's house and hauled the sunfish onto the lawn. A rag-tag parade of aunts, grandmas, and little kids marched down the street from the Country House to see the prize. Everyone marveled.

Everyone, except Great Grandma. She took one look at the sunfish and shook her head.

"Dig a hole. Bury it!" she commanded in Sicilian.

"But Grandma, it is such a big fish. Something could be eaten."

"No. Bury it."

"Is it poisonous?" asked Uncle Tom.

"No. Bury it in a deep hole so it doesn't infect the garden." said Great Grandma. She stomped off back to the Country House.

"If it's not poisonous," reasoned Uncle Tom to his daughter-in-law, Marsha, "something could be eaten."

As it turned out, the sunfish yielded a very small amount of flesh. The meat was white and looked clean, but Uncle Tom boiled a piece, just in case it was poisonous. Uncle Tom and Aunt Marsha handed out a taste for all of the onlookers. Within seconds burning pin and needle sensations invaded their tongues and lips. The pain could not be washed away with water or beer. The whole sunfish was buried in an extra deep hole, away from the garden and grape arbor.

I imagine Great Grandma had known sunfish. She grew up in Casetellmarre de Golfo, a fishing village along the Sicilian coast. Since sunfish eat only jellyfish, their small amount of meat is inedible, and, according to Great Grandma, not even worth fertilizing the garden.

BAKING BASS, BLUES, AND BLOWFISH

Blowfish were an easy catch and abundant in the Great South Bay on the south shore of Long Island. They were everywhere—along the piers, in the seaweed grassland, and in a million secret fishing holes.

My daughters enjoyed fishing for blowfish.

Dad would fasten a small hook at the end of a string for each little kid in our tremendous brood. He taught us to bait a hook with a shiner we caught in seining nets earlier in the day. We threw our lines over the dock or boat railing. The first big lesson was to remember to hold onto the other end of the string. In no time, (it must have been within seconds because I do not remember any of my siblings or cousins with an attention span that lasted more than a minute), a tiny shake, a tug, and finally a pull brought up a buck-tooth blowfish.

Bluefishing was exciting and required a boat ride to the inlet, heavier poles, reliable reels and sharp hooks. Striped bass, however, was the prize of a fishing expedition. These beautiful fish offered a delicate white meat that did not require a good deal of fuss to prepare.

Nonna called striped bass spindella, because of its strong dorsal fin. She opened the whole fish flat on a baking dish, sprinkled her bread crumbs on top and a generous drizzle of olive oil. She folded the fish back together and popped it into a 350° oven. Dad said that Nonna liked to keep the head on, but Grandma Truglio insisted the heads be buried with the guts, since she did not like to look at the eyes.

Bluefish, a gamier meat, needed additional attention. Grandma Truglio shook salt and pepper on top, added bread crumbs and onion slices then wrapped it in foil to bake in a 350° oven or on a charcoal grill.

Blowfish tasted better than any chicken nugget (they were not yet invented when I was a kid). Grandma Truglio sprinkled salt, pepper, and bread crumbs on the blowfish tails, generously drizzled olive oil on top, and baked them in a 350° oven until brown. They were quickly devoured with a side of ketchup.

1969 Dad and Billy Boy

III

EGGPLANT

9

PARM & STACKS

Eggplant is a family favorite. When properly cooked, eggplant lends itself perfectly to just about any dish. Fried eggplant slices are a staple in my home. I didn't realize how much so until my daughter, Sara, felt compelled to get herself an eggplant tattoo with "MA" scrolled under it. I suppose every generation has its way of honoring their elders.

Eggplant is a nightshade vegetable. It can compliment many medleys and bring its own savor to the table. It can also stand alone grilled, fried, or baked. For all of its virtues, eggplant requires patience. Before committing to eggplant, one must plan and prep. It is one of those foods that holds a high bar of excellence.

Grandma Truglio cooked a hands-down master eggplant parmesan. She learned to cook alongside her mother, Nonna, and followed her secrets, style, and taste to become an accomplished home cook. My dad, Grandma's oldest son, contends that although his mother could cook anything into a culinary masterpiece, Nonna was the high commander master cook of any dish that came out of the narrow 6x10 kitchen on East 5th Street in Brooklyn. Some crowns cannot be relinquished.

In my memory, Grandma's eggplant parmesan will always be best. I strive to replicate but never hit the mark. Grandma peeled the dark skin on the eggplant and somehow sliced long thin slices without the aid of a mandolin. Because eggplant meat is porous, she bathed the slices in salted water for a little while. Salty water draws out and dries the eggplant so that the oil does not soak in as much when it is fried. Once the eggplant was pat dry, Grandma dredged the slices in an egg wash and then into bread crumbs. She pan-fried them in a generous amount of very hot olive oil.

Once golden brown, the fried slices were transferred onto a paper bag that was ripped flat open so the oil would drain. The slices were then layered with mozzarella cheese, her hearty sauce and grated parmesan cheese in a Pyrex glass pan. It was baked in a 350° oven until the cheese melted and the edges bubbled. Grandma sopped up the excess oil along the edges with a paper towel and let the dish cool for a few minutes to "set" the cheese.

Grandma's eggplant parmesan was heaven over macaroni. The eggplant was tender enough to cut with a fork and long stretches of cheese had to be twirled on a fork. Grandma's eggplant parmesan made incredible cold or hot sandwiches, too.

Back in the day, food was not considered the cause of heart disease or diabetes. Meals were created out of what was available for the day. No one could afford to be picky.

Today's home cooks try to recreate beloved dishes with wise choices. I attempted to tone down the fat, cholesterol, and calorie intake of my eggplant dishes. Although an admirable goal, it was not easy to sacrifice taste and comfort.

When Grandma first struggled with diabetes and cholesterol, everyone tried to accommodate her diet. I made her ground turkey meatballs with egg whites, wheat germ and a splash of marinara sauce on top. She graciously took a bite, thoughtfully chewed and swallowed. She pushed the plate towards me and said, "So, this is good for you."

I attempted to adapt the eggplant parmesan recipe by lightly seasoning thin slices of eggplant and brushing the tops with oil. I broiled them to a brown hue, then stacked with meatless sauce and low-fat mozzarella cheese. Although the reduction of fat and cholesterol was significant, this healthy version was not even close to what I wanted to accomplish. My motto now is "Cholesterol Be Damned—I'm frying my eggplant!" Consequently, I save fried eggplant for special occasions.

Like so many of the hand-me-down recipes, evolution and taste preferences adapt the preparation. Personally, I like the purple black skin on the eggplant. It adds a pleasant bitterness. My mom's stuffed eggplant keeps its skin. When grilled, the eggplant skin around the slice caramelizes a bit and holds the delicate meat in place. But, not everyone is an eggplant skin fan. I compromise and peel the eggplant so that the big bulb looks like it's wearing striped pajamas.

I adapted Grandma's delicious eggplant parm into eggplant stacks. They are a big family hit. Even my dad will admit that it is almost as good as his mother's eggplant parmesan.

Grandma Truglio and most of her grandchildren

Eggplant Stacks

EGGPLANT STACKS

1 to 2 eggplants that are firm (calculate for extra slices since there will be kids who will want a rolled slice as a snack, and others may want a stack to bring for the next day's lunch.)

- salt
- 2 eggs
- bread crumbs
- olive oil
- tomatoes
- mozzarella
- basil leaf

Peel (or not peel) the eggplant and cut into thin round slices. Lay two layers of paper towels on a board and sprinkle with salt. Arrange the eggplant slices on the paper towels, salt and cover with another layer of paper towels. Continue until all of the eggplant is salted and covered. Place a heavy board on top to weigh them down and help squeeze the water out. Let them sit for 30-45 minutes.

Slice the tomatoes and cheese. Rinse the basil leaves. Set aside.

Whisk eggs and a splash of water to make the wash. Put the bread crumbs in a dish next to the eggs.

Remove the weight and paper towels from the eggplant slices. Pat the eggplant dry with a clean paper towel.

Heat the olive oil in a heavy pan. The oil should be about a ½ inch deep.

Dip an eggplant slice in the egg wash then cover with bread crumbs. Carefully place the eggplant in the hot olive oil. When each side of the eggplant is golden brown, place on a plate lined with two layers of paper towels.

Here is the hard part. Fend off anyone wanting to test, snack or save themselves from starvation.

When all of the slices are fried and pat dry, it is time to stack them. Place a bottom layer of eggplant in a baking dish. Add a tomato slice, basil leaf and mozzarella slice. Top with an eggplant. You can make another layer or simply put a basil leaf and piece of cheese on top.

Make a foil tent over the pan so the cheese does not melt to the foil. Bake in a 350° oven for 20 to 25 minutes.

10

CAPONATA

Caponata is another family favorite featuring eggplant. Grandma said that she prepared caponata to cook all of the vegetables that had been in the refrigerator too long. I would imagine that this was not the case with my first generation mamas. An icebox or refrigerator was not available, so each day a mama or nonna went to the market. They bought just enough for the day because there was no way to keep the food from spoiling. This must have been quite the chore, especially in the summer months when everything and everyone wilted in the heat.

Refrigeration technology and speedy truck and rail deliveries provided a means for fresh foods to travel further and keep longer even during the hottest days. The disadvantage to such wonders is that food could be forgotten. I confess that my zucchini has languished in the bottom refrigerator drawer and a piece of fennel could sit in the corner of a shelf beyond its life expectancy. Happily, they may not be wasted when incorporated in caponata.

Caponata varies from cook to cook and from the individual cook herself. My mom cooked up a big batch as a Sunday appetizer and had enough left over for lunches. At work, I was assigned to bring my caponata for the potluck days.

The recipe may look like a lot of work but it really is a matter of cooking down a pile of chopped vegetables and adding herbs and olives.

Some caponata ingredients

CAPONATA | 49

Eggplant Caponata

EGGPLANT CAPONATA

- garlic
- olive oil
- eggplant
- salt
- celery
- fennel
- onion (red or yellow)
- peppers (use a red or orange pepper for a pop of color)
- tomatoes
- mushrooms
- zucchini
- yellow squash
- oregano (fresh or dried)

- thyme (fresh or dried)
- diced tomato in 14.5 oz can
- ½ to 1 cup of vegetable broth
- pesto
- ~2 tablespoons balsamic vinegar
- green olives
- freshly chopped or dried parsley
- pine nuts (optional)

Put a head of garlic in foil and drizzle at least 1 tablespoon of olive oil on top. Wrap loosely and roast in a 400° oven until the cloves are soft (about 40 minutes).

Peel (or not peel) the eggplant. Cube and salt the eggplant and spread them out on a pan. Place paper towels on top of the cubes and a heavy board to press out the liquid.

In the meantime chop the celery, fennel, onion, peppers, tomatoes, mushrooms, zucchini, and yellow squash. I like to scrape the seeds from the zucchini and yellow squash—my preference. Season with just a bit of salt, ground pepper, oregano, and thyme.

Heat a big frying pan and add 2 tablespoons of olive oil with a sliced garlic clove. Stir until fragrant.

Pat the eggplant dry and put into the pan. Cook for 5 minutes or so. Add the chopped vegetables into the pan. Stir in the pesto with two or more sliced cloves of roasted garlic. Stir, adding olive oil if necessary.

Stir and cook for five minutes or so. Add the can of diced tomatoes. Continue to stir and cook evenly. Do not let the vegetables stick to the bottom of the pan.

Add the vegetable broth and drizzle balsamic vinegar into the vegetables. The amount of vinegar depends on your taste preference. Splash a little and taste. You can always add. Stir and let most of the liquid cook down until the vegetables are at a desired texture.

Add the olives, parsley, and optional pine nuts. Stir. Let cool.

You can store the caponata in an airtight container. It tastes even better the following day. Serve cold with whole wheat crackers or slices of bread.

Mom cooking, again

11

UNCLE TOM'S HEARTBURN

Uncle Tom was everyone's favorite. He was part of the Truglio family long before his son, Jack, married my dad's cousin Marcia Truglio. As a child, Jack lived down the street from the Country House and cavorted with the cousin posse. Although kids have a way of making their own fun, Uncle Tom was their enabler of boat shenanigans and summertime play. He had the know-how, tools and imagination to teach, mostly the boys, how to keep a flimsy fleet of boats running for their fishing, crabbing, and water skiing adventures. Uncle Tom could fix almost anything with just about nothing.

I knew Uncle Tom as a surrogate grandfather since both of my grandfathers passed before I was born. When I was a kid, Uncle Tom permanently moved from New York City to Long Island. He commiserated with my dad and uncles to keep boats floating and working all for the goal of providing everyone fun family days.

As Uncle Tom got older, his drive for a good time did not waiver. He tweaked boat engines to make them go faster, got crowds up to dance (the Chicken Dance was his favorite), and was always included on all the escapades. Actually, Uncle Tom instigated most of the escapades.

When I was a kid, my mom and aunts told us to play outside. My cousins and I walked to Uncle Tom's from the Country House to find tackle and some semblance of a crab net, or borrow a boat. Uncle Tom usually tagged along, speeding in the channels, whipping a water skier too close to the shore or a buoy. He let us climb to the top of his roof and jump or dive into the canal, clearing docked boats by just a smidgen.

Age did not deter him through his 80s and 90s. He lived with his son, Jack, in Maryland and frequently traveled, visiting his grown grandchildren in California, and drove to see his older sister in Rhode Island and us on Long Island. He liked the mild winters in Florida and enjoyed celebrating birthdays or anything else on a sailing trip in the Virgin Islands with his family. He loved a party. Uncle Tom was never far from the action and strived to be the big kid in the room.

Uncle Tom was an accomplished home cook in his own right. His mother had a macaroni business when he was a child. Being the youngest and the only American-born child of his family, he probably spent a lot of time watching and helping his mother. Uncle Tom also took good care of his very ill wife, Aunt Josie, and managed domestic duties. His sister, Aunt Kate, five years his senior, was a frequent visitor, helping him organize his home and care for Aunt Josie. For a Sicilian man of his generation, he navigated the kitchen well.

Uncle Tom enjoyed his fish and macaroni dishes. Of course, he didn't write anything down. Uncle Tom invented his version of pickled eggplant and called it *Heartburn* because of the spicy herbs.

Pickling and canning vegetables was a common practice for most immigrant families in the early 20th century. Stone crocks and worn wine barrels served as pickling vessels. Just about all foods could be preserved with salt and vinegar and whatever spice a native palate desired.

Fond memories of Uncle Tom continue through the years. His full belly laughs with a soggy cigar clenched between his teeth and his hand pushing a throttle of a recently restored boat engine are relived at family gatherings, on boats, and around the table.

Uncle Tom and Dad on a boat

UNCLE TOM'S HEARTBURN RECIPE

- eggplant
- 2 cups of white vinegar
- bay leaf
- red pepper flakes—about ½ teaspoon more or less depending on your taste
- half a head of garlic—peel and cut the cloves in half
- 1 teaspoon of olive oil
- 1 thinly sliced onion (optional)

Peel every bit of skin off the eggplant. Use a very sharp knife, mandolin, or a potato peeler to cut the eggplant into thin strips—about a half-inch wide. Salt the strips and distribute on a board with paper towels under and over the strips. Place another board on top and let it sit for about 30 to 45 minutes. If you are adding onions, salt and press them with the eggplant.

Combine the vinegar, bay leaf, red pepper flakes, and garlic into a small pot. Simmer for 5 to 7 minutes. You should be able to pierce a garlic easily.

Loosely pack the eggplant strips (and onions slices) into glass jars meant for canning. Pour the hot vinegar concoction into the jars. Remove the bay leaf. Seal. Give the jar a little shake to distribute the garlic and pepper flakes. Store in the refrigerator for a few days before taste testing.

Uncle Tom's Heartburn is a welcome addition to a cold antipasto dish or on thick slices of bread.

Uncle Tom

IV

VEGGIES, EGGS, AND A SANDWICH

12

CONVERTING THE CAULIFLOWER SHUNNERS

Cauliflower is a hard vegetable to like. The smell of cauliflower cooking permeates through the house with that "cauliflower" aroma. Either you love it or hate it. In my cauliflower taste preferences, a middle ground is possible only if the pale flowers are soaked in a vat of pickling vinegar or buried in batter and fried.

Aunt Antoinette cooked a cauliflower dish in red wine that was brewed by her brother-in-law, Uncle Frank. Winemaking in basements, and later, garages, was part of many Italian-American homes. The men usually took on the grape selections, pressing, bottling, and bragging rights.

Uncle Frank

My great grandfather was a champagne grape grower in Sicily, toiling for the landlord. Although he did not farm in America, he did have a barrel in his basement and made wine for home and bartering purposes. I have vague memories of my great grandfather, but the aroma of fermenting grapes remained in the basement many years after his death.

In my memory, Uncle Frank was the most prolific family winemaker. His whole house smelled like fermenting wine. It was easy to get drunk just by breathing. My cousin, Sal, at age 17, would take the shop's truck with Uncle Frank to the Brooklyn Terminal Market. Uncle Frank would take a bunch of grapes out of a crate and taste test. If he didn't like the grapes, he would put them back. If he liked them, he would slap the crate, signaling for Sal to take it. Uncle Frank bought red and white Moscato grapes. Sal loaded at least one hundred cases into the truck and drove to Uncle Frank's house on Long Island.

Uncle Frank called his style "Symphony Wine," probably because, after a glass or two, singing and playing pianos and mandolins were inspired well into the early morning hours. Each year Uncle Frank pressed and bottled 200 gallons of a rosé blend. The wine aged a few short months rather than long years. When Uncle Frank came to the table or a party, a few Symphony Wine bottles filled many glasses, and extra bottles were gifted to the hostess. Some sauces and favorite dishes also featured Symphony Wine. When the wine turned, it made for flavorful vinegar.

Today, Aunt Joann, Aunt Antoinette's daughter, regularly cooks her mother's cauliflower recipe, converting those who shun cauliflower. I will confess, with an extra portion of olives and cheese, I can enjoy cauliflower.

CAULIFLOWER IN UNCLE FRANK'S SYMPHONY WINE

- head of cauliflower cut into bite-size florets
- 1½ to 2 cups of red wine (a chianti or cabernet sauvignon works well)
- olive oil
- green olives chopped
- garlic chopped (2-4 cloves)
- salt and pepper to taste
- chunks of parmesan, Locatelli, or Grana Padano cheese or grated cheese

Put all of the ingredients except the cheese, salt, and pepper, in a pot. Cover and simmer until the cauliflower is tender (about 10-15 minutes). Stir gently to distribute the wine without breaking the florets. Add more wine if more liquid is needed.

Remove from heat and gently stir in the cheese, salt, and pepper. If you add a lot of cheese, you will not need salt. Serve hot with a glass of red wine.

Uncles taste testing the wine.

13

BREAD CRUMBS

Bread crumbs were born from the stale bread slices and unwanted crusts. Many dishes, especially vegetable dishes, are sprinkled or coated with bread crumbs. It is a pantry staple. Modern grocery stores and corner bodegas routinely stock various brands, flavors, and styles of bread crumbs.

Great Grandma did not buy canisters of bread crumbs seasoned or unseasoned. She saved leftover pieces of bread, allowed them to go stale, scraped off any mold that may have started to grow, and finally grounded, seasoned, and stored the staple ingredient. Dad reported that Nonna also collected and grounded old bread. Still, Grandma Truglio, my mom, and aunts forfeited the messy and tiresome chore and kept store-bought bread crumbs already seasoned and ready to coat and sprinkle on their favorite foods.

Just like cleaning ash from the kitchen coal stove and hand-washing laundry in a tub with a scrub board, homemade bread crumbs faded from the weekly chore list. Great Grandma, the last holdout for any technology, did not give in to advancements without skepticism and a good fight. She insisted on washing laundry her way even when a washing machine was neatly installed in the basement. Instead of taking advantage of the voluminous refrigerator space, Great Grandma walked to her favorite markets to buy only what was needed for the day. She shrugged on her black coat, tied the kerchief under her chin, placed her pocketbook in the crook of her arm, and headed out to the Brooklyn streets. Her age did not deter the routines. In my memory, I witnessed her scrub sheets in a tub and hung clothes on lines. Great Grandma made her breadcrumbs.

When she traveled out of Brooklyn to visit my family on Long Island, she had several missions. The first was to give each of her five great-grandchildren a good shake to ensure our sturdiness, and a toothless kiss on each head. Although she had lived in America for over 70 years, she only spoke Sicilian but understood English perfectly. My siblings and I dutifully nodded and smiled at her ramblings. She wandered into the gardens with my mom beside her, agreeing to the Sicilian directives for growing the vegetables and flowers. Mom understood her perfectly.

After the tour, Great Grandma put on her apron and called her great-granddaughters to attention.

"Dalla!" she demanded, meaning, "Watch!"

My dad or an uncle had already ground the stale bread (I think this was regulated as a man's job). Great Grandma made me and my sisters stand around the kitchen table. She ripped a paper grocery bag flat and slapped it on the table. The ground bread was dumped on the flattened bag.

Great Grandma

"Dalla!" she repeated, shaking a warning finger not to touch.

Great Grandma took handfuls of crumbs between her open palms and rubbed, letting a rain of crumbs fall into a golden mountain. She then made a shallow well in the middle of the mound. Salt, pepper, and the dry trinity—parsley, basil and oregano—filled the well. She drizzled fragrant olive oil in and around the well. The rhythmic waves of the palm mixing mesmerized my sisters and me, tempting a hand reach.

"Dalla!" Hands quickly retreated. Great Grandma had a swift slap.

Great Grandma continued to rub the mixture between her hands, adding a shake of salt, a pinch of oregano, and another splash of olive oil. She never tasted. Satisfied with the bread crumbs' feel, smell and look, Great Grandma took the edge of the paper bag and funneled the bread crumbs, now well seasoned, into a big glass jar. Once she tightened the lid, my sisters and I dispersed. Lesson over.

I must confess that I never made breadcrumbs. Leftover bread crust and stale slices float in thick soups or are fed to the ducklings in the canal. However, the memory of my forceful great grandmother rubbing crumbs and firmly stating "Dalla!" are conjured when I open a canister of store-bought bread crumbs.

Great Grandma and her daughters

ROASTED VEGETABLES

- fresh vegetables: onions, fennel, peppers, mushrooms, zucchini, yellow squash, tomatoes, and 2 or 3 cloves of garlic
- olive oil
- salt and pepper to taste
- dried or freshly chopped trinity (basil, oregano, parsley)
- bread crumbs

Preheat the oven to 400°. Slice the vegetables and season with salt, pepper, and the trinity. Toss in the olive oil. Lay the vegetables in a cookie pan. Bake in the oven for 30 minutes, until the vegetables are tender and a bit brown. Sprinkle with breadcrumbs. Put the pan of vegetables back in the oven for 5 minutes until the tops brown.

A Sunday dinner

14

ARTICHOKES

Grandma Truglio served the stuffed artichoke course at the grown-up table after a large dinner. A bowl of nuts with never enough nutcrackers also appeared as the artichokes were distributed. It was a kind of an intermezzo, but not really. Artichokes and nuts were not meant for palate cleansing. It was more like an intermission where the pace of eating and conversing could slow down just a bit. The artichoke and nut course offered everyone a chance to nibble on something and sip the last of the wine while the dishes were being washed. It also gave those who planned to come for just cake and coffee an excuse to snack on something savory before a sweet.

I often wondered how civilization decided that this prickly bud was worth the time and effort to domesticate. It can be an unfriendly food with its tough leaves and prickers. Artichokes are the immature flower of a thistle, so that it is technically not a vegetable. However, in the culinary world, artichokes are treated and prepared as if it were a true vegetable. It is certainly one of those toughees that is worth the labor. Artichokes contain an abundance of antioxidants, aid digestion and lower blood sugar. Grandma must have known an artichoke was exactly what we needed after a heavy meal and before a table of treats.

Grandma's artichokes were large deep green flowers swollen with crisped breadcrumbs. By the time artichokes came out of the kitchen, we kids had finished our dinner at the kids' table. We milled around the grown-up table looking to sit on a lap, tattle, or try our hand at cracking the walnuts with the nutcracker. Grandma liked to share her artichoke with the kids. She let us pull the outside leaves from the flower base. We scraped our teeth on the leaf's underside to eat the baked stuffing that was seasoned with garlic and Parmesan cheese. As the deflowering continued, the stub of the leaf became tender and added another layer and flavor to the artichoke experience.

Soon a plate was piled with teeth-tracked leaves until, finally, the choke revealed itself. Its pale leaves, tipped with a faint hue of purple spikes stood up. The breadcrumbs had not made it to this deep end of the flower. Grandma pulled the naked artichoke towards her.

"You don't like this part," she'd say and ordered us kids to go play. It was fine with us since the fun was over and, by that time, our attention was directed elsewhere.

I may have been in high school when I remained at the table to watch Grandma finish her artichoke. She easily pulled the choke from the base and scraped the fuzz with a spoon to get to the heart. The grey-green heart did not look appetizing. Grandma split it with her fingers and popped a piece into her mouth.

"The best part," she'd say. She was right. The heart was absolutely delicious. It was tender and tastier than the tough leaves and held more flavor than any jarred artichoke heart.

Why go through the mess just to get to this small yet incredible part of the artichoke? I imagined Grandma thought the effort spent at the table with the kids helping her eat the artichoke was the delicious journey to the heart.

Grandma Truglio and two of my sisters

Stuffed Artichokes

STUFFED AND BAKED ARTICHOKES

- artichokes
- bread crumbs
- garlic powder
- Parmesan or Pecorino cheese
- olive oil

Cut the stem off the artichoke and trim the pinchy tops with heavy scissors or a sharp knife.

Put in enough water at the bottom of a pot so that the artichokes can steam. Steam for at least 40 minutes until an outside leaf can be pulled off without too much trouble. Run cold water over the artichokes.

Mix seasoned bread crumbs, garlic powder and Parmesan or Romano cheese.

Spread the leaves out as much as you can. Use a spoon to stuff as many breadcrumbs in between and into the center of the artichoke.

Place the artichokes in a baking dish. Drizzle olive oil on top. Loosely place aluminum foil over the artichokes.

Bake in a 300° oven. After 40 minutes remove the foil. Bake until the tops are a little crisp. The outside leaves should easily pull up off the base.

Serve with a glass of wine and a conversation.

A kids' table

15

BREAKFAST WITH GREAT GRANDMA

Great Grandma did not have an appetite for cooking, being one of those who did not revere food. Food was like air, simply necessary, and not her expression of love and creativity. She let her pristine home, garden, and master needlework express her heart.

Eggs were her go-to protein and always yielded a quick meal. Each morning, Great Grandma prepared herself a soft-boiled egg, a slice of day-old Italian bread, and thick coffee. My sister, Mary, and I remember the very soft boiled eggs. We had to sleep over Great Grandma and Grandma Mastropaolo's house in Brooklyn because the other Grandma's joyfully noisy five-room flat was too full of little sisters, a baby brother, and visiting cousins. Being the eldest, I was big enough to sleep over in the orderly house on West 9th Street, but I needed to drag a sister with me. I convinced Mary, one year younger than me, that sleeping over this Grandma's house was a big kid privilege—Mary believed me.

The night was long and lonely. We were sent to bed with freshly brushed teeth and a kiss on the forehead soon after my parents left with the younger kids. Great Grandma and Grandma Mastropaolo lived together on the first floor of the house. They made good use of the basement to store jars of food and do laundry by hand, and the upstairs apartments supplemented their income.

Everything about Great Grandma's house was clean. Not a speck of dust took up residency on any surface. The bare wood and mosaic-tiled floors shined, and the bedsheets were tighter then the most meticulous soldier could have done. Mary cuddled up next to me in Grandma's bed and quickly fell asleep. For me, sleep was always hard to surrender to, even at six years old. I listened to the outside traffic, hoping to recognize a car brake or rumble signaling that my daddy had come to take us back to 2202 East 5th Street. As the night wore on, I succumbed to the fact that Grandma Mastropaolo's shrill insistence that we prove our favor to her, dismissed any hope of an escape.

Great Grandma rose early in the morning and peeked in to make sure we were still sleeping. I usually wasn't. She directed me to follow her and be quiet. Great Grandma did not speak English and my Sicilian vocabulary consisted of "No!" and "Aspetta! (Wait)" but, with her hand gestures and firm tone, there was little chance of a translation error.

I sat in a chair next to the chrome table in the kitchen while Great Grandma put a small pot of water and the coffee pot on the hot stove. She set the table in the dining room while I sat and watched the pot. Three eggs were placed in the boiling water. Once the coffee percolated, the eggs were done. I think Great Grandma's 3-minutes was a little faster than the standard. She had a full day ahead of her, and there was no time to wait on eggs. The eggs were taken off the heat and showered under cold water. I followed her to the dining room, where my sleepy five-year-old sister waited.

The eggs sat, narrow side up in the prettiest little egg cups. Great Grandma cut slices of day-old Italian bread and poured herself a cup of coffee. Mary and I had a glass of milk with our hard bread and soft egg. There was no reason to whine for Sugar Frosted Flakes or Froot Loops. They would not be in the pantry.

According to Great Grandma, nobody tapped an egg, peeled eggshell, and removed the top of an egg as skillfully as she. No matter our finger grip on a demitasse spoon, or our gentle taps, Great Grandma took our spoons, demanded our attention while she tapped, peeled, and removed the top. She spoon fed us the first bite. Mary would sit back and stick her tongue out with bits of googy egg white, but I, being a wiser one year older, knew better and swallowed the egg without gagging.

Great Grandma dipped her bread in the black coffee and then into the liquidy egg innards, softening the stale bread so that she could manage with her lonely three teeth. I couldn't say I dipped my bread in milk and then into the egg, but I do remember taking tiny spoon sips of the yolk to earn an approving head nod. I took solace that Daddy and Mommy would soon pick us up and we would have buttered toast and Cheerios covered in sugar at Grandma Truglio's house.

Dinner at Great Grandma's

SOFT-BOILED EGGS

- eggs

Bring a small pot of water to boil. Gently place eggs into the pot and cover. Time the boil for a solid three minutes (I would suggest four minutes).

Remove the eggs from the boiled water and run under cold water.

When cool to the touch, place the eggs in a pretty little egg cup. Some shot glasses work well, too.

Tap the shell, peel, and pull the top to reveal the soft yoke.

16

SEAMLESS SANDWICH

When I was a brand new mom, I enjoyed bringing my baby girl, Sara, to the grocery store. I'd tucked my infant into a front knapsack carrier and push a shopping cart up and down the familiar aisles. When she grew out of the carrier, I lined the shopping cart with thick blankets. Those handy-dandy infant seats that snap out of the car seat base and fit neatly in the shopping cart seat were not yet invented. I needed another cart to pull around for the groceries. Once Sara was big enough to sit up safely, I was happily reduced to one cart.

I started the excursion at the bakery. If I timed the shopping just right, I could pick out a warm, crusty, freshly baked loaf of Italian bread. It was Sara's favorite. I pulled the heel off the loaf (my favorite) and gave the bread to Sara. She dug into the soft insides with her little hands and happily ate as we shopped. She reached her whole arm into the loaf to pull every bit of fluffy bread. The long loaf was hollowed out by the time we paid the cashier.

I had a loaf of Italian bread prepped for the next favorite dish—a seamless sandwich. I am not sure who invented and termed the hearty food a seamless sandwich, but it certainly lived up to its name.

Without a slice down the middle and the insides pulled out, the bread loaf could hold the sandwich contents with minimal fallout.

Back in *Daily Bread* days, I imagine that my great grandfathers, grandfathers, and great uncles carried a lunch pail to work. Their meal probably contained a half-loaf seamless sandwich filled with a savory leftover. In my memory, Aunt Kay stuffed cold cuts in a seamless loaf and packed the sandwiches in lunch coolers for fishing trips and beach excursions. Grandma Truglio somehow lined the insides with thick slices of mozzarella cheese and filled the bread with meatballs drenched in sauce.

The best seamless sandwich memory was when Great Grandma and Grandma Mastropaolo came to take care of my siblings and me for four days. My parents were on a trip (I think it was the first and last trip they took time for themselves). I was in the fifth grade, and my youngest sister, Barbara, was in first. My three sisters and I walked to school and stayed in school for lunch for those few days. My four-year-old brother stayed home all day with the Grandmas, nodding to their Sicilian banter, pretending to understand.

The thing to know is that when you brought lunch to school, there were incredible options to trade sandwiches, fruit, and snacks. I usually had a salami sandwich—hold the mayo and mustard. Although salami was my go-to sandwich filler, I coveted peanut butter and jelly between two soft slices of Wonder Bread. There was always a friend or two willing to trade a half salami sandwich for half of a peanut butter and jelly. Sometimes, I scored a Drake's Yodel for a whole sandwich and my three Oreo cookies.

Great Grandma had other lunch menu plans. She scrambled eggs with leftover fried artichoke hearts and onions, stuffed the warm concoction into a quarter loaf of Italian bread, and wrapped the seamless sandwiches in foil. After carefully arranging the sandwiches, a soft peach swaddled in a napkin, and a cookie she baked the day before into four brown paper lunch bags, we were shooed out of the house for a day of learning.

There was a reason why the artichoke hearts and onions were leftover from the previous night. Being kids under the age of ten, we had little appreciation for the delicacy. No one wanted to trade my seamless sandwich, and the mushy peach could not be negotiated. I nibbled on the plain cookie.

Barbara found me on the playground.

"What did Grandma pack you for lunch?" she asked.

"Artichokes and eggs," I replied.

"Uhh! Me, too. I bet Billy got pastina for lunch."

Now that we are all grown up, a scrambled egg with leftover artichoke hearts and onions stuffed in a crusty loaf of Italian bread makes a fantastic lunch or dinner. Trade negotiations are no longer necessary.

SEAMLESS SANDWICH

- leftover vegetables that were breaded and fried or sautéed
- olive oil
- 2 to 3 eggs
- long loaf of Italian bread
- grated cheese (optional)
- salt and pepper to taste

Reheat the vegetables in a pan with a dash of oil to keep food from sticking. Scramble the eggs and add to the vegetables in the pan. Add salt and pepper to taste. Cook until the eggs are firm. Remove the pan from the heat.

Cut the loaf of bread in half width-wise. Pull out the soft insides. Don't worry. Someone will eat it.

Carefully stuff the eggs and vegetables into the hollow loaf.

Wrap the seamless sandwich in foil. You can heat it, making it a tasty hot lunch, or dig in to it cold. Both ways are delicious.

V

SOUPS AND STEWS

17

VERSATILE CHICKEN SOUP

Residents in the Little Italy section of New York City, 1911, did their daily shopping from peddler carts. Vendors set up shop on the sides of the streets, selling everything from apples, sewing needles, nuts, and tin cups. Fish, chickens, beef and pork were also sold from the carts. The vendors would load their wares early in the morning to entice buyers with their fresh bargains. Women did most of the shopping, bartering, and filling their bag with the day's catch.

When my families migrated out of the tenements to Brooklyn, neighborhood shops supplied them with everything they could ever need. However, there were some remnants of the old ways. Dad remembers the scissor man rumbling down the street offering to sharpen knives, the givel man who sold bleach, brown soap and lye, and the fish monger who rode through neighborhoods on Wednesdays and Fridays.

The matriarch of the household had her favorite bread shop, butcher, and grocer. Most of these essential stores were in the neighborhoods. However, Great Grandma did not consider the close proximity of her preferred shops. She went to merchants she liked and whom she could speak to and bargain with no matter how far the walk.

As a little girl, my mom remembers holding onto her grandmother's hand while walking briskly down 86th Street to Avenue X in Brooklyn, not too far from Coney Island. Livori's chickens pecked at bugs and grain behind a chain linked fence. Her grandmother picked out the chicken she wanted, negotiated price, then turned back to her neighborhood to finish the rest of the day's shopping. Later, still holding hands, the pair returned to the poultry man and picked up the chosen chicken, plucked and gutted.

This was a weekly excursion. Mom remembers how fast she had to trot alongside her grandmother, firmly holding her hand, while they walked through the crowds.

Great Grandma roasted the prize and prepared chicken stock from the carcass, gizzards, heart, and liver. The rich stock became the base for chicken soup.

Like chicken, chicken soup has a variety of versions—chicken soup with rice, chicken noodle soup, chicken soup and dumplings, cream of chicken soup. The list is endless. Nonna and Grandma Truglio thickened their chicken soup with wide macaroni. Great Grandma plopped small meatballs in her chicken soup, but her favorite was chicken and escarole soup.

In today's world, chickens are sold in clean packages, ready to cook any way you want. To accommodate busy families, grocery stores also sell seasoned and roasted rotisserie chickens ready to eat for less money than buying a raw roaster. Chicken broth is on hand in boxes and cans. I confess to buying a roasted chicken from the grocery store. The meal is delicious and plentiful. If time and motivation allows, I will cook down the carcass with carrots, celery, and an onion. I do not miss adding the heart or liver, and picking through the gizzards. More often than not, though, boxed chicken broth fits into my schedule and satisfies my chicken stock needs. It is a good enough shortcut. Progress. I do imagine Great Grandma and Grandma Truglio making the comment that my shortcut is just that—a shortcut.

VERSATILE CHICKEN SOUP | 89

Great Grandma in the kitchen with Aunt Bea and Grandma Mastropolo

CHICKEN BROTH

Fill a stock pot with about 8 cups of water. Add the chicken carcass, stalks of celery (include the tops) whole carrots, onions with skins cut in quarters, peppercorns, salt, and fresh or dried trinity (basil, oregano, parsley). Bring the pot to boil and simmer for an hour or so. Strain the bones and vegetables from the liquid. Pick the meat from the bones and set aside. Let the pot sit in the refrigerator for several hours or overnight. A layer of fat will surface and solidify. Remove as much as desired. The stock can be kept in the refrigerator for a few days or frozen.

CHICKEN SOUP WITH ESCAROLE

- olive oil
- garlic chopped
- bay leaf

- onion chopped
- carrots sliced
- celery stalks sliced
- chicken stock
- 14.5 oz of diced tomatoes
- cooked chicken meat
- salt, pepper and dried trinity
- escarole washed and torn

Drizzle oil in the soup pot. sauté garlic and bay leaf until fragrant. Add onions, carrots, and celery and sauté until the onions are almost transparent. Pour in the chicken stock and diced tomatoes, and add the chicken meat. Season to taste. Bring the pot to a boil then simmer for 30 to 40 minutes. Check the seasoning. Before serving, bring the soup to a boil, and add the torn escarole. Boil about 5 minutes or until the escarole is tender and reaches a desired texture. Serve with crusty bread and or grated parmesan cheese sprinkled on top.

"STICK TO YOUR RIBS" COMFORT

The proper Italian term is *pasta fagioli*. The Neapolitan and Sicilian pronunciation is *pasta fasule*. *Pasta fazool* is Brooklyn-ese made popular by Dean Martin singing *That's Amore*.

Basically, pasta fasule is a bean soup with pasta cooked in it or served over a pasta. The soup is often thick, a bit creamy, and aromatic from herbs and hardy stock. Pasta fasule packs protein and complex carbohydrates that fuel the body.

Beans were a mainstay staple for my great grandparents' lives in Sicily. In their tenement homes, dried cannellini, pea and lentil legumes were cheap and could be stored in jars and crocks. These non-perishable foods provided a large family nutritious meals.

Hot pots of pasta fasule welcomed everyone home on bitter nights. It soothed cold days and "stuck to your ribs," satisfying physical and emotional hunger. It is the ultimate peasant comfort food. During the autumn and winter, my mom cooked up lentils in vegetable-based stews. A cannellini bean medley included sweet sausage or leftover chicken. Steaming hot mugs of split pea with ham soup satiated lunch.

When she ladled the soup or stew on top of rigatoni or linguini, a hearty supper was completed.

Family, 1959

Lentil Stew Over Spaghetti

LENTIL STEW

- 1 cup of dried lentils
- 6-8 cups of water
- olive oil
- 1 bay leaf
- sliced garlic
- onion chopped
- carrot chopped
- celery chopped
- 14.5 oz can of diced tomatoes
- season with salt, pepper, dried parsley, basil, oregano, garlic powder
- vegetable stock as needed
- linguine or spaghetti
- grated Locatelli cheese (optional)

Soak the dried lentils in 2 cups of water for an hour or so. Rinse and set aside.

Heat a drizzle of olive oil in a pot, and simmer garlic slices and bay leaf until fragrant. Add the chopped onion, sliced celery and carrots. Season with salt, pepper and red pepper flakes. When the onions are a bit transparent, add lentils and diced tomatoes. Season with the trinity—basil, parsley, and oregano. Simmer for a few minutes.

Add 4 cups of water and let the stew cook down uncovered until the lentil texture is to your liking. If you want it a little more soupy, add a cup or two of broth or water. Served over linguine or spaghetti. Grated Locatelli cheese makes a tasty garnish.

Family, 2020

"STICK TO YOUR RIBS" COMFORT | 97

Split Pea Soup

SPLIT PEA SOUP

- 1 cup of dried split peas
- 4-6 cups of water
- ham steak or leftover ham bone
- garlic
- bay leaf
- onion chopped
- carrots sliced
- celery sliced
- salt, pepper, and dried trinity: oregano, basil, parsley
- chicken stock
- rigatoni

Soak the dried split peas in 2 cups of water for an hour or so. Rinse and set aside.

Heat a drizzle of olive oil in a pot and sear the ham steak. Cut the ham in bite sized pieces. Simmer the chopped onion, sliced celery and carrots with garlic. Season with a pinch of salt (the ham is very salty) pepper, and red pepper flakes. When the onions are a bit transparent, add the split peas and ham. Add 4 cups of water or chicken broth and a bay leaf.

Let the soup simmer and cook down until the peas are soft. Add more water or broth if you like the texture looser. You can pulse an immersion blender to smooth out the peas and vegetables. Be careful not to blend too much of the ham.

Serve the split pea soup on top of rigatoni or offer pasta-less with a crouton garnish.

Sisters in the kitchen

Pasta Fasule

CLASSIC PASTA FASULE

- 1 cups of dry navy or cannellini beans
- 4-6 cups of water
- garlic
- olive oil
- red pepper chopped
- onion chopped
- carrots sliced
- fennel sliced small
- 14.5 oz can of diced tomatoes
- chicken or vegetable stock
- sweet Italian sausage, cooked chicken or cooked beef (cut the meat into bite-sized pieces)
- salt, pepper, and dried trinity: oregano, basil, parsley
- tubetini or other small pasta

Soak the dried beans in 2 cups of water for an hour or so. Rinse and set aside.

Heat a drizzle of olive oil in a pot, simmer garlic slices and bayleaf until fragrant. Add the chopped onion, sliced carrots and fennel. Season with salt, pepper and red pepper flakes. When the onions are a bit transparent, add beans and diced tomatoes. Season with the trinity —basil, parsley, and oregano.

Simmer for a few minutes. Add meat (optional). Stir in 4 cups of water or stock and let the soup simmer and cook down until the beans are tender. Add 1 ½ to 2 cups of broth so that the soup is watery enough to cook 1 cup of the small pasta. Served with grated cheese.

Sunday dinner, 1966

VI

DESSERT

WHAT'S FOR DESSERT?

Ready for dessert? It doesn't matter if you are not hungry. There is always room for a treat.

Sunday dinners ended with table clearing to make room for dessert. Coffee cups and small dessert plates with freshly cleaned forks were distributed. A bottle of anisette appeared, ready to spike the black coffee (aka espresso). White bakery boxes were untied and opened. When I was a kid, there was always a little squirmish about who got the bakery string (I needed all the cat's cradle practice I could muster since my Brooklyn cousins were masters). Cannolis, a fruit pie, and a cake in the chocolate family from the corner bakery were the regulars.

A few homemade treats also adorned the tables. My mom baked the chewiest brownies and sticky sweet upside-down pineapple cake from boxed cake mixes. Aunt Lil brought her cheesecake and apologized for the crack on the top. We quickly made that error go away by slicing it up and eating it first. Recently, my niece, Eileen, has sharpened her pastry chef skills and creates beautiful tarts, cakes, and vegan specialties with the help of her two little boys.

Special occasions called for traditional treats. There was pumpkin pie for Thanksgiving, Italian ices for the 4th of July. Mom's Christmas cookies not only looked festive but were so delicious. Everyone had their favorite. If there was a birthday nearby, Carvel's ice cream cake was lit up with candles and swiftly shared.

St. Joseph's Day is a Roman Catholic holiday celebrated by many Sicilians. The story goes that a severe drought plagued Sicily in the Middle Ages. The people prayed to St. Joseph, the patron saint of the home, and Jesus' selfless stepfather and Mary's husband, to bring the rain to their crops. In return, they promised a big feast to commemorate his legacy. Right on cue, rain showered down, and a holiday was born.

St. Joseph's Day is celebrated each year on March 19th. It marks the end of winter, the beginning of spring, a worthy reason for something sweet. It was common for Sicilian immigrants' birthdays to be recorded on a saint's day. Great Grandma claimed St. Joseph's Day as her day. Being one with no real record of an actual birth date in 1880 Sicily, she could claim any saint's day as her birthdate.

In the Daily Bread story, Papa's birthday was on St. Joseph's Day and a cake to celebrate the day was necessary. St. Joseph's Day cake is a battered dough baked then stuffed with a cream filling and topped with a cherry. In the tight kitchens of the Lower East Side tenements, 1911, maraschino cherries may not have been available, but I imagined a piping bag was fashioned in some way and a sweet creme was whipped up. Perhaps a dollop of strawberry preserves topped the cake.

My cousin, Andrea Manfrede Simmons, is a baker in her own right. For over 30 years, she has been the proprietor and master chef of Andrea's Cheesecakes in Orlando, Florida. She graciously shared her version via email.

From: Andrea Simmons

Sent: Sunday, September 6, 2020, 2:05 PM

To: Antoinette

Subject: St. Joseph's Cake

I have to admit I have not made these in years, but still have the recipe.

The recipe is similar to the zeppole that I make every year for Easter Sunday. My family looks forward to it every Easter, as it is not the same without them!

Baking with my grandaughter

ST. JOSEPH'S CAKE

This yields about 16 pastries

Dough

- ½ cup butter
- 1 ½ teaspoons sugar
- 1 cup water
- 1 cup flour
- 4 eggs (room temp)

Melt the butter, sugar, and water in a saucepan until it comes to a boil.

Add the flour and stir until it forms a ball.

Beat the eggs one at a time and add to the dough until the mixture is smooth.

Put in a piping bag with a large star tip and pipe a Rosette on a pan with parchment paper.

Make a hole with the back of a spoon for the filling and Bake for 20 to 30 minutes at 400 degrees or until golden brown.

While the cream puffs are baking, prepare the filling.

Filling

- 2 egg yolks
- 2/3 cup milk (room temp)
- 5 oz. sugar
- 2 ¼ tablespoons cornstarch
- pinch of salt
- 1 teaspoon vanilla extract
- powdered sugar
- maraschino cherries

In a small pot, add the egg yolks, sugar, corn starch, salt, vanilla, and whisk.

Turn the burner on low and slowly pour the warm milk while whisking, gradually increasing the heat. Cook until the mixture thickens about 5 minutes or so.

Poke a hole in the side of the pastry.

Use a piping bag to fill the inside of the pastry and swirl it over the top. Sprinkle with powdered sugar and top with a cherry.

Good luck with your new venture. I look forward to the memories.

Love,

Andrea

20

MRS. GOLDBERG'S KNOT SURPRISES

Mrs. Goldberg, the baker's wife, is a fictional character in my middle-grade historical novel *Daily Bread*. To 9-year-old Lily, the protagonist, Mrs. Goldberg, is a magical ballerina with glittering cheeks and an artist's heart. Although Mrs. Goldberg and her loving baker husband struggle to make ends meet in Manhattan's crowded Lower East Side neighborhood, 1911, simple acts of kindness eventually save the bakery and Lily's family.

My grandmother did not have a recipe for Knot Surprises. She baked pies and gorgeous bread and rolls but never wrote down her baking secrets. Instead, I experimented in adapting bread recipes my mother used to create my version of Mrs. Goldberg's Knot Surprises. Be mindful that I am not an accomplished baker. Like a chemistry lab exercise, one must follow directions, and pay attention. I barely passed required chemistry classes—saved only by my smart choices in lab partners. While making up the Knot Surprise recipe, I had a few baking mishaps (my finger burns are healing nicely), but, with the help of my talented niece, Eileen Snyder, this version worked out best.

Mrs. Goldberg's Knot Surprise

MRS. GOLDBERG'S KNOT SURPRISES

- 1 package of active dry yeast
- 1½ teaspoon salt
- 2 teaspoon sugar plus a little extra for sprinkling
- 3-5 cups of flour
- 1 cup of warm water
- oil or soft butter
- egg and a splash of water to create an egg wash

Surprise Filling:

- melted butter, 1:1 mixture of cinnamon and sugar mixed together to create a paste or
- jam or 1 teaspoon of honey

Stir the flour and salt together. Use a measuring cup to mix the warm water, yeast and sugar. Gently stir until the sugar and yeast dissolve.

In a separate bowl, mix the sweet yeasty water with 2 cups of flour. Stir until the flour is smooth. Add flour until the mixture is well incorporated, and the dough pulls away from the sides.

On a board dusted with flour, knead the dough, adding sprinkles of flour until your hands come clean.

Place the dough back into the bowl. Brush with oil or soft butter. Cover the top of the bowl with a clean towel. Let the dough rest and rise in a warm spot.

When the dough is almost twice its original size, knead out the air. Cut and roll palm-size balls. Shape the balls in a long oval.

Spread a dollop filling in the middle of the oval. Roll the oval longwise, twist and knot. Place the knot on a parchment-lined pan. When all of the knots are on the pan, brush them with the egg wash and sprinkle with sugar. Let stand for 30-45 minutes. Bake in a preheated 350 degree oven for 18-20 minutes (about).

Helpers

ACKNOWLEDGMENTS

This project proved to be a joy. Despite my amateur culinary style and even more anemic food photography skills, I loved collecting and compiling family stories and favorite dishes that made *Becoming America's Food Stories*.

The most influential voice in *Becoming America's Food Stories* were my parents, Bill and Diana Truglio. Their stories held a treasure trove of memories of their grandmothers and mothers in the kitchen, growing up in Brooklyn, and their adventures with boats, holidays, and meals while raising their family.

I also tapped into my uncles and aunts' reminiscences—my parents' peers for fun, adventure, and nourishment. Great big thank you shout-outs go to Uncle Phil Stagliano, Aunt Ursula and Uncle Mike Buono, Aunt Joann Estes, Aunt Linda and Uncle Vic Truglio, Aunt Tosca Manfrede, and Aunt Marcia Triolo. Sincere gratitude also goes to my sister, Diana Yanoti, who helped authenticate many of the recipes. She inherited our grandmother's bread-baking hand and cooked braciole our father claimed to be almost like Nonna's—an excellent compliment. My cousin, Andrea Simmons, and niece, Eileen Snyder, deserve thanks and applause for helping me with the two deserts. They rescued me from my poor attention to measurements and time in baking anything beyond a boxed cake mix. Special thanks go out to my cousin, Larry Manfrede, who provided repaired and colorized photos of our families.

Sara Martin, my incredibly talented daughter, guided and patiently instructed me on the basics of staging and photographing food. This was a steep learning curve for me, but Sara leveled the challenges and managed to instill a fair bit of confidence for me to accomplish the task. Thank you. Thank you.

Beta readers are essential to any book's journey. I was so fortunate and grateful to Nicole Cuddihy and Christine Flaherty. These fine ladies were ready and willing to critically read the manuscript and reflect within a tight timeline.

Stephanie Larkin and the incredible staff at Red Penguin Books brought *Becoming America's Food Stories* to the world. I am thankful for their indulgence and patience as the book came into its own.

Finally, big bear hug thanks go out to my husband, Matt. He cheered me on and happily ate the successful and the not so successful recipe attempts with no complaints.

ABOUT THE AUTHOR

Antoinette Truglio Martin wrote *Daily Bread* from the stories her grandmother, aunts, and mother told around the dinner table. Antoinette is also the author of the memoir *Hug Everyone You Know: A Year of Community, Courage, and Cancer* (She Writes Press) and the children's picture book, *Famous Seaweed Soup* (Albert Whitman and Company). She proudly holds an MFA in Creative Writing and Literature from Stony Brook/Southampton University, had several essays published in journals, and wrote regular columns for local periodicals. As a retired educator, she now conducts author visits in the schools and professional development seminars for teachers. Check out her blog, *Stories Served Around The Table*, where you can find a bevy of family tales and life's musings.

https://storiesserved.com/

https://www.facebook.com/AntoinetteTruglioMartin2017/

https://twitter.com/StoriesServed

www.ingramcontent.com/pod-product-compliance
Lightning Source LLC
Chambersburg PA
CBHW050327120526
44592CB00014B/2084